A DrNurse
Publishing House

New Orleans, Louisiana

COPYRIGHT ©2019 by Dr. Scharmaine Lawson and its licensors.
All rights reserved.

Book Design and formatting by Uzuri Designs

No part of this book may be reproduced or transmitted in any form or by any means, electronic or mechanical, including photocopy, recording, or by any information storage and retrieval system without the written permission of the publisher or author except where permitted by law.

For information address A DrNurse Publishing House
PO Box 56572, New Orleans, La. 70152
www.NolatheNurse.com

ISBN-13: 978-1-945088-25-4

LCCN: 2019941807

Author Contact info:
DrLawson@DrLawsonNP.com

www.DrLawsonNP.com
www.NolaTheNurse.com

Nola the Nurse®

Explores S.T.E.M. Activities

Volume 7

by Dr. Scharmaine Lawson NP

Illustrated by Marvin Alonso

Our Body

THE HUMAN BODY

Parts of the Body

Connect the dots to see the full picture.

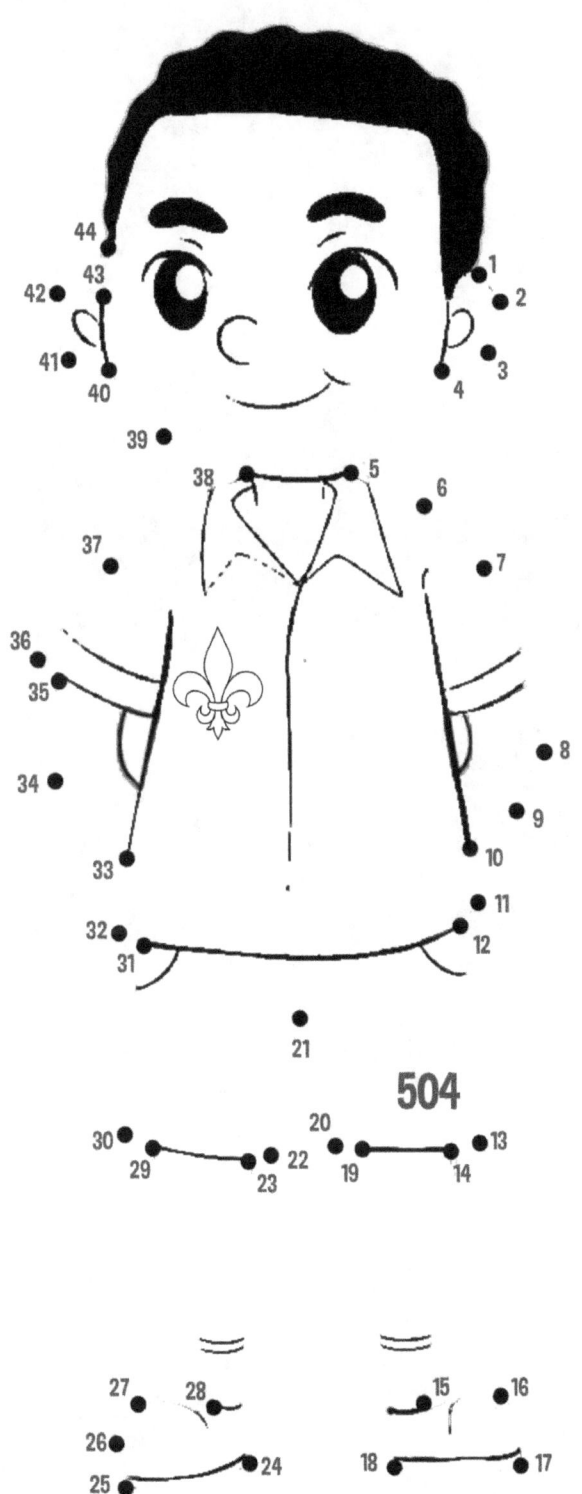

504

www.nolathenurse.com

Write the name of each body part on the line.

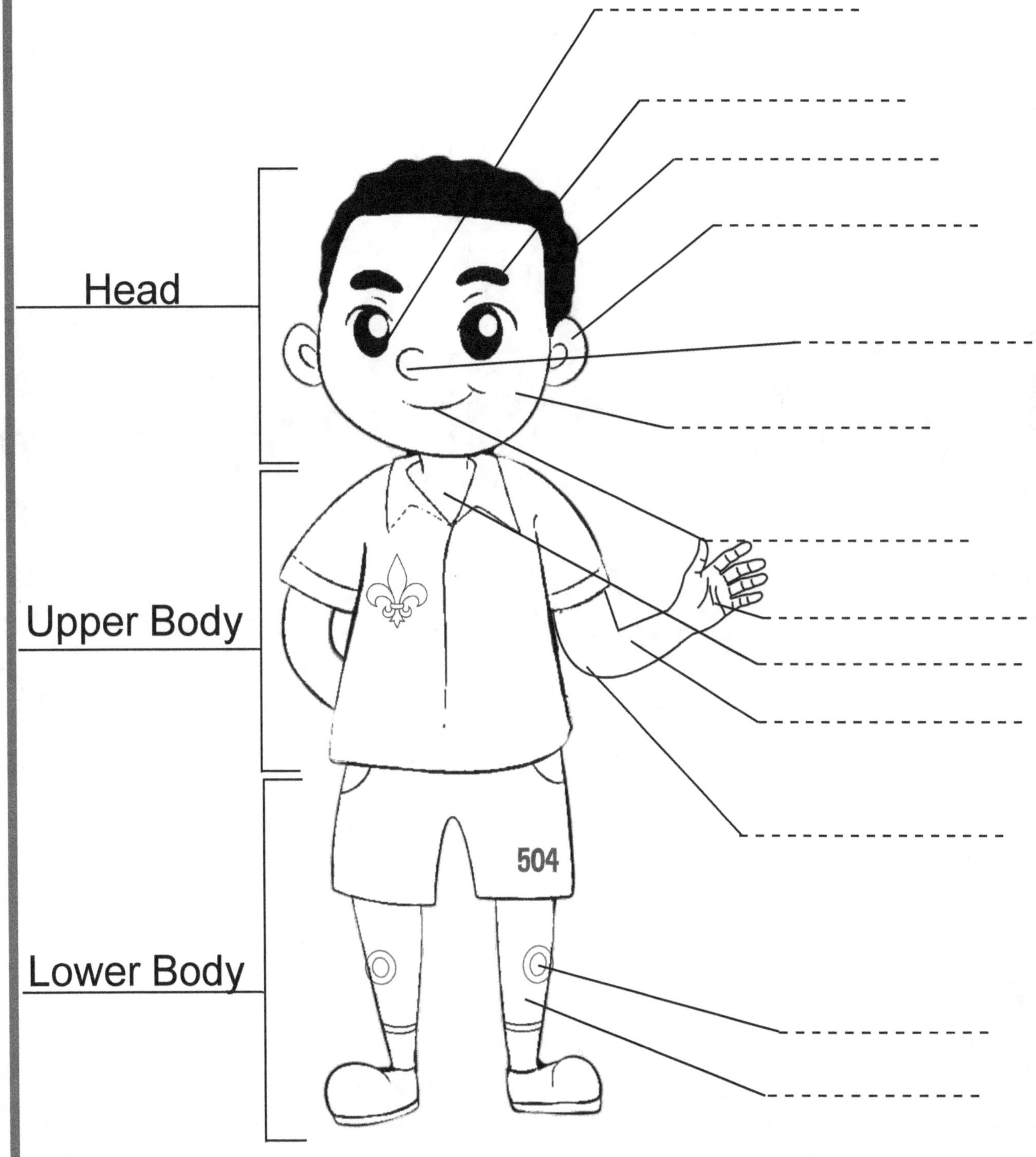
Head
Upper Body
Lower Body
504

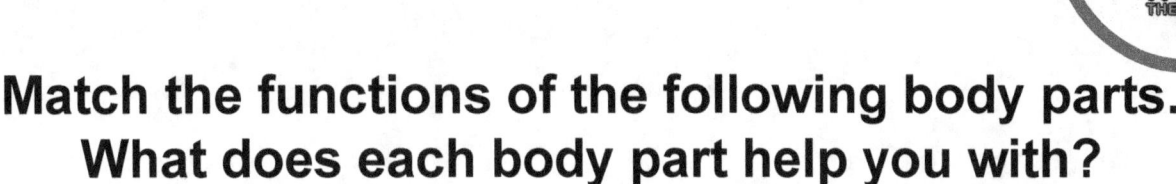

Match the functions of the following body parts. What does each body part help you with?

Arms

These are at the end of the legs and help us to walk, run and stand.

Neck

These are at the end of the arms and help us to pick up things.

Feet

This allows you to move your head from side to side.

Tongue

These are used to chew food.

Hands

These are limbs that help us to walk, run and stand.

Teeth

These are limbs that help us to pick up things.

Legs

This helps us to taste food.

Draw or trace your hand in the space below:

Answer the following questions:

- How many hands do you have?

  _____

- How many pairs of hands do you have?

  _____

- How many fingers do you have on one hand?

  _____

- How many fingers do you have in total?

  _____

- Do you have fingernails?

  _____

- Are your fingernails long or short?

  _____

- Are your fingernails clean?

  _____

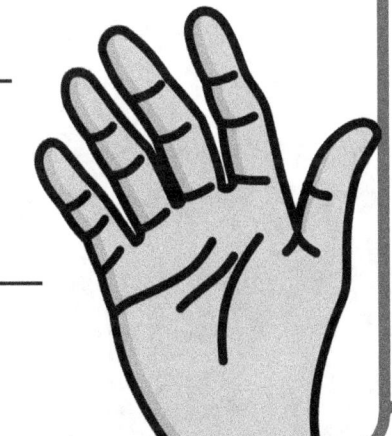

www.nolathenurse.com

Fill in the blanks with the correct word.

Our body has three parts, the _____ , _____, and lower body.

The _____ has the _____ and fingers. The _____ connect the _____ with the upper body.

Head   Upper Body   Arm   Neck

Hands   Shoulders   Arms

Look at your reflection in the mirror. Identify the parts of your face and draw your face in the space below:

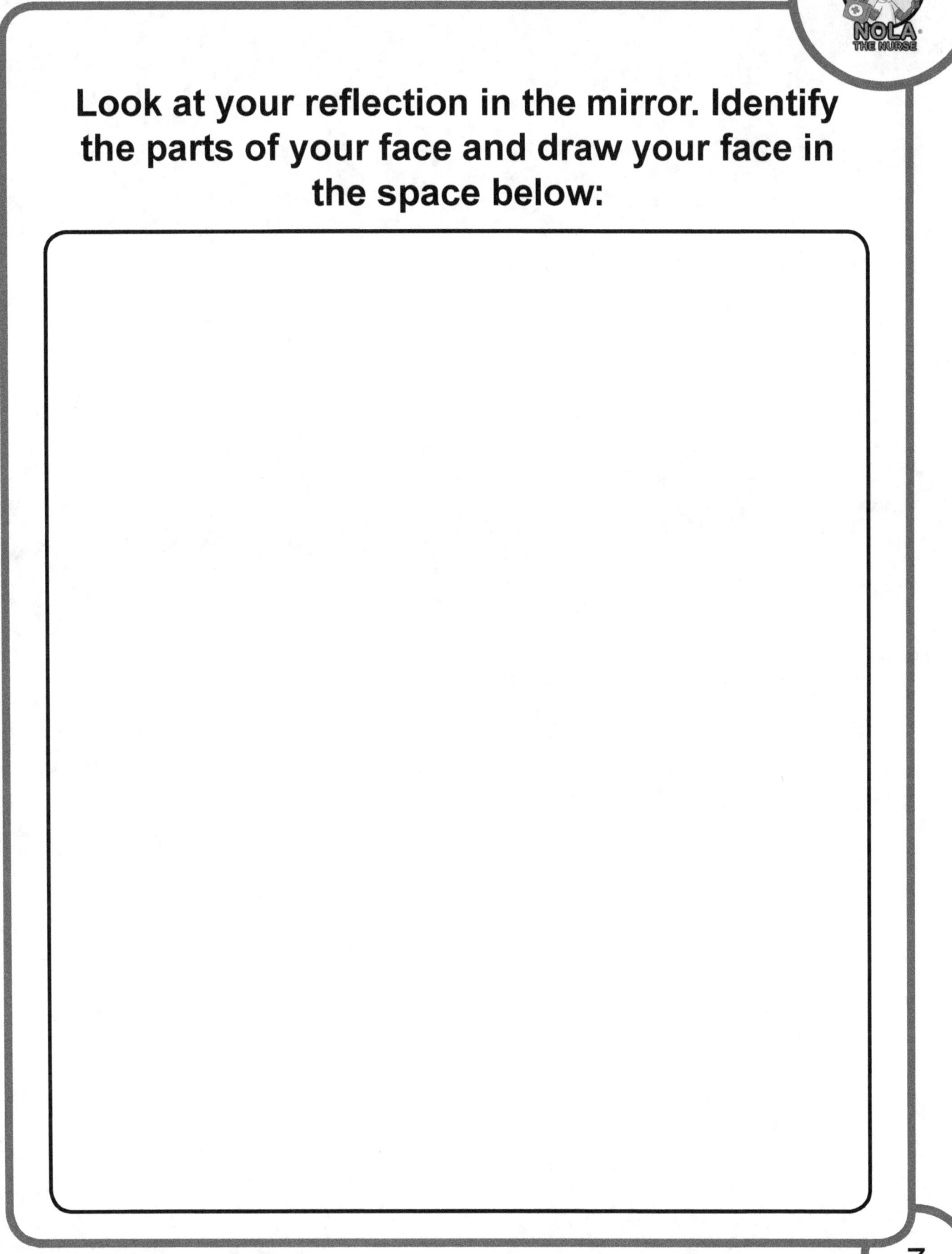

Circle the correct answer. Which of these can you do with your hand?

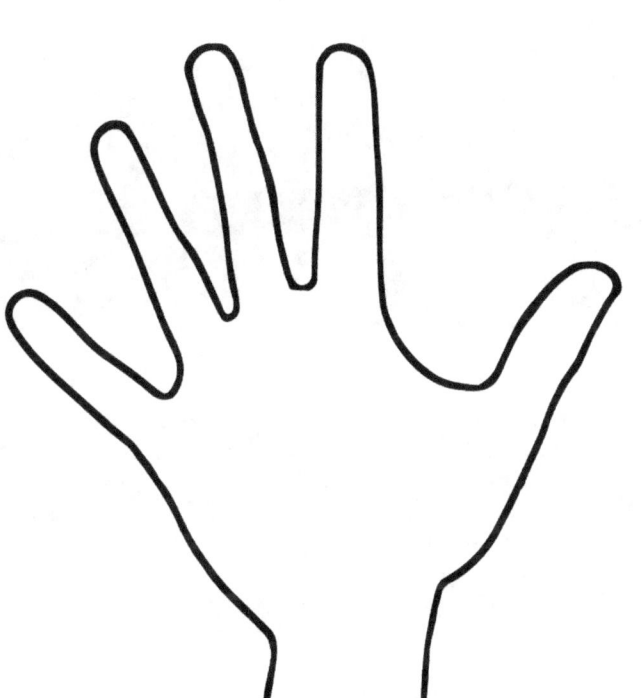

Touch

Write

Eat

Draw

Hear

Kick

www.nolathenurse.com

Circle the correct answer. Which of these can you do with your leg?

Hop

Walk

Eat

Drink

Talk

See

Run

Jump

Fill in the spaces with the missing letters.

   _ o _ e

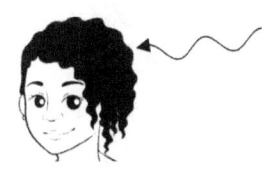   H _ i _

   _ ong _ e

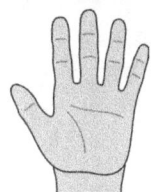   F _ n _ _ rs

   F _ _ t

   E _ e

   _ e _ k

   M _ u _ h

Read this information about the skin to answer the questions on the next page.

Let's learn about another very important organ, the skin. The skin is the largest external organ of the body.

The skin covers our entire body and it has a lot of functions. One of its functions is to protect us from the outside environment, keeping the bad stuff out of our body and keeping the good stuff inside our body.

The skin is also a sense organ. It helps us feel when we touch something. We can tell if something is hot when we touch it. We can feel if something is cold when we touch it.

The skin is considered the largest organ of the human body.

The skin has 3 main layers. They are the: Epidermis, Dermis and Hypodermis.

www.nolathenurse.com

THE SKIN

Questions

1. What is the largest external organ of the body?

   _____

2. How many layers does your skin have?

   _____

3. What are they?

   _____

4. What does the skin help you with?

   _____

   _____

   _____

Our Body

THE HUMAN BODY

What's inside our bodies?

Label the organs shown in the diagram below:

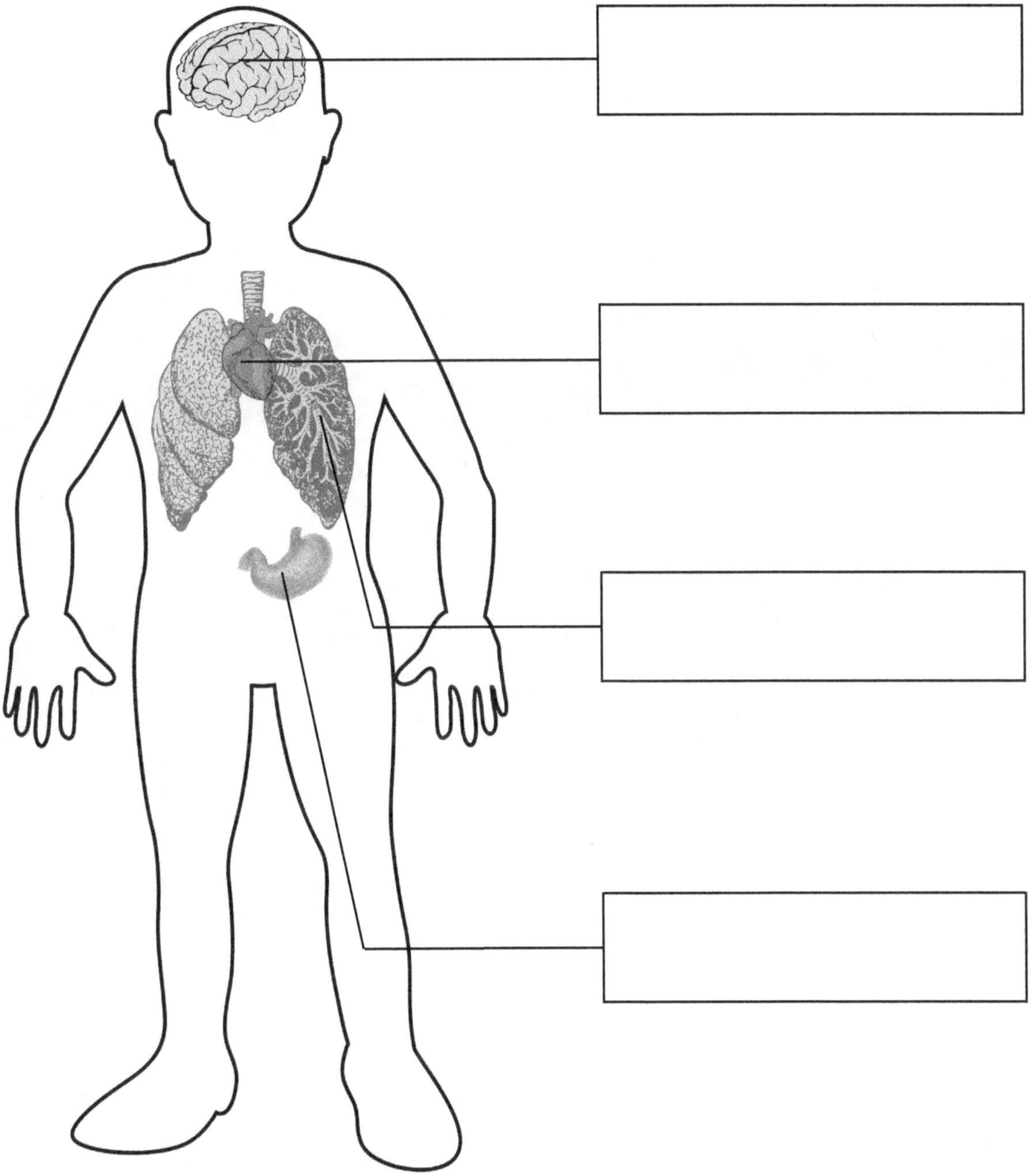

Match the functions of the following organs. What does each organ help you with?

Heart

Helps us to breathe

Lungs

Turns the food we eat into energy

Brain

Pumps blood to all parts of the body

Stomach

Help us to think and do good things

Connect the dots to see the organ below:

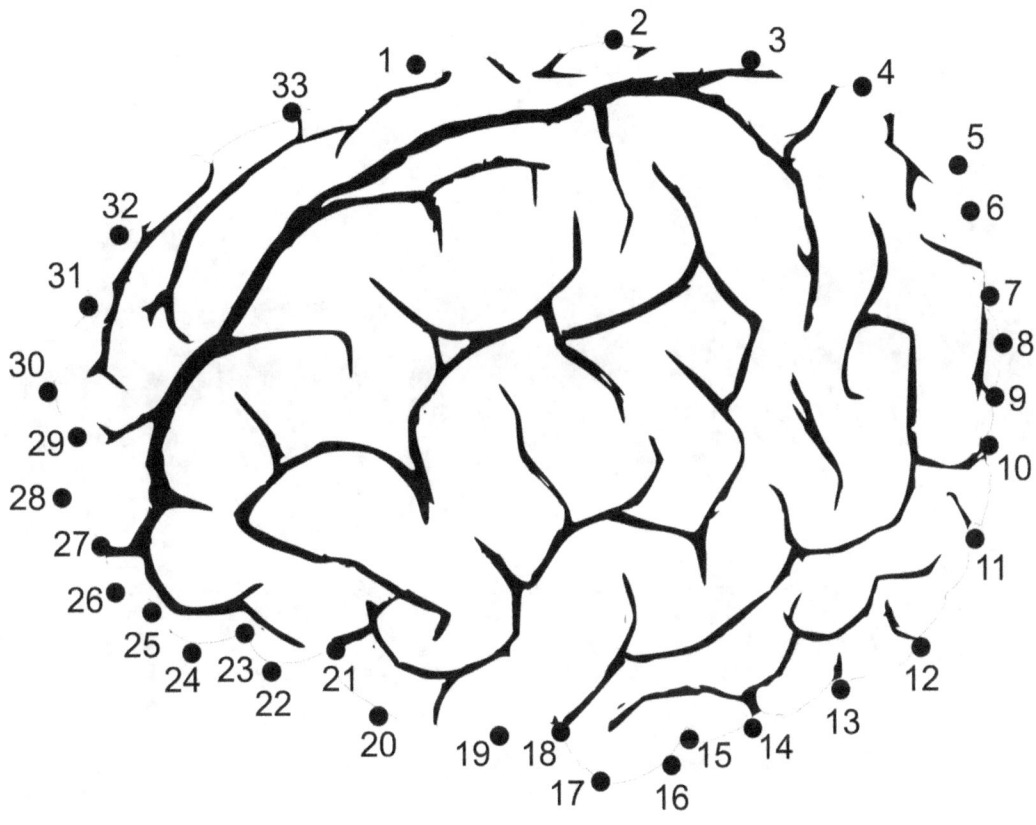

Which organ is this?

_____

Connect the dots to see the organ below:

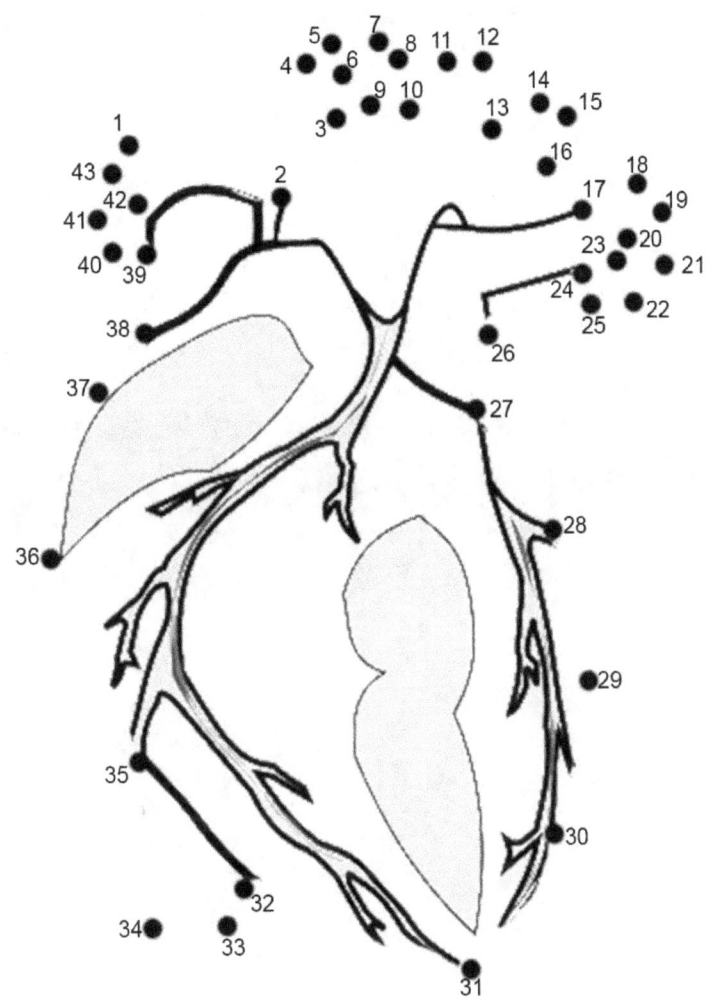

Which organ is this?

_____

Connect the dots to see the organ below:

Which organ is this?

_____

Connect the dots to see the organ below:

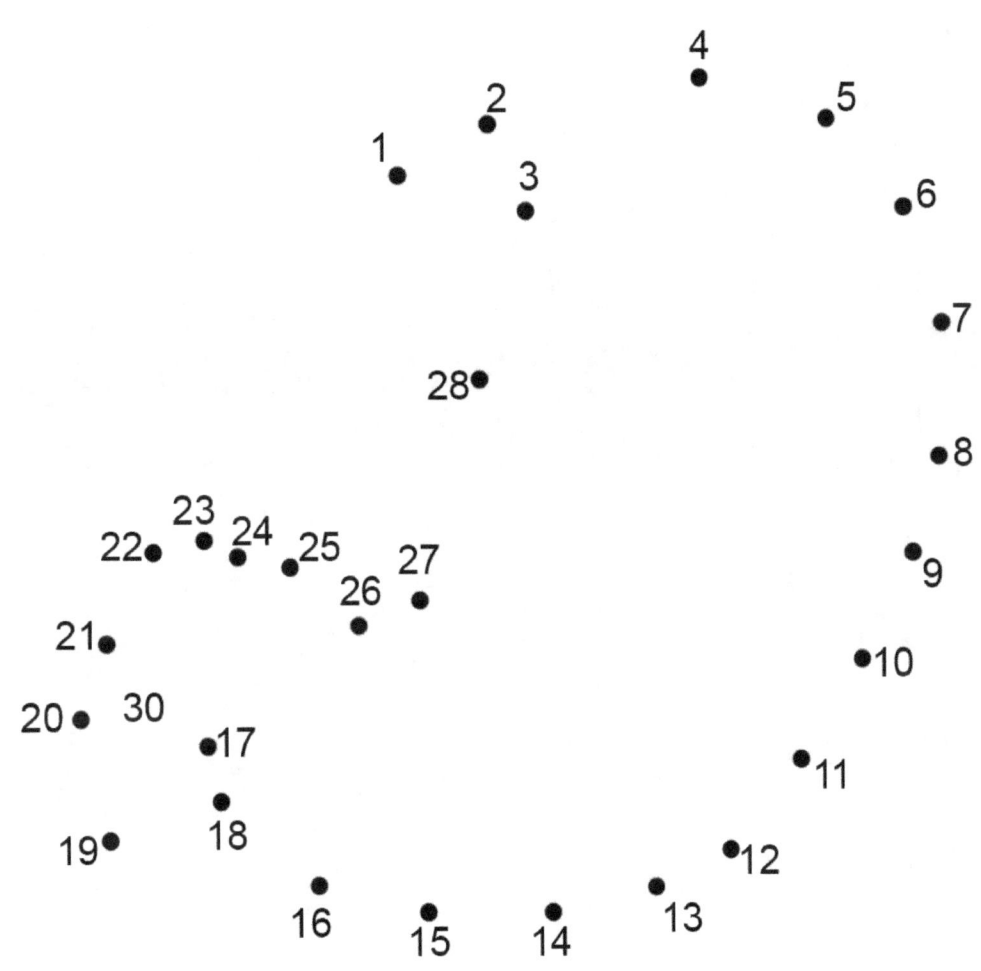

Which organ is this?

_____

Alice ate some food. The food Alice ate has to travel to the stomach to be converted into energy. Can you draw the path the food has to take to enter Alice's stomach?

www.nolathenurse.com

Do you remember all the outer body parts you learned? Can you list them?

_____

_____

_____

_____

_____

_____

_____

_____

_____

Charo The CRNA

Do you remember all the inner body parts you learned? Can you list them?

Read the paragraph below and write True or False next to the statements below:

Blood is the red stuff that oozes out when you bruise or cut yourself after a fall. We cannot live without blood. Blood carries oxygen and nutrients to all the cells in your body for you to grow and stay healthy. Your blood carries waste products away from your cells to keep your body clean. Blood fights germs that enter your body to help you get better when you are sick. Your heart pumps blood to help it travel all around your body.

Blood is a liquid. _____

Blood is blue in color. _____

Blood travels all around our body carrying oxygen and nutrients to cells. _____

Blood does not carry waste products away from cells. _____

Blood helps us keep our body clean. _____

Without blood we cannot survive. _____

Blood helps you fight germs that get into your body. _____

www.nolathenurse.com

Circle the correct answers.

1. What is the color of blood?

Blue   Green   Orange   Purple   Red

2. The _____ pumps blood all around the body.

Lungs   Brain   Stomach   Heart

3. Blood helps us to:

Fight germs   Eat food   Think

Carry things to and from our body cells

Our Body

THE HUMAN BODY

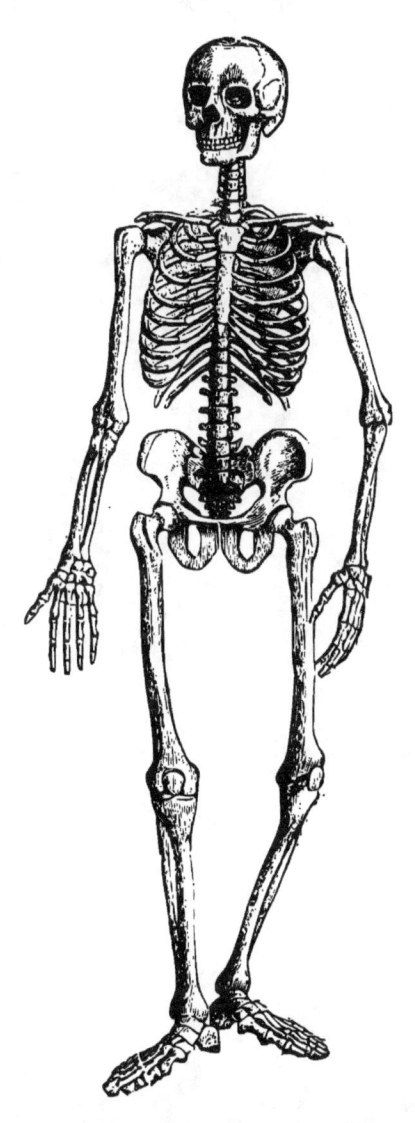

Bones

Read the paragraph below:

Your body has a definite shape. Your bones keep your body parts together in place. All 206 bones in your body together form the skeleton which gives your body its shape. The point where two or more bones meet is called a joint. Joints help us bend our body. Can you bend your elbow? That is because of the elbow joint.

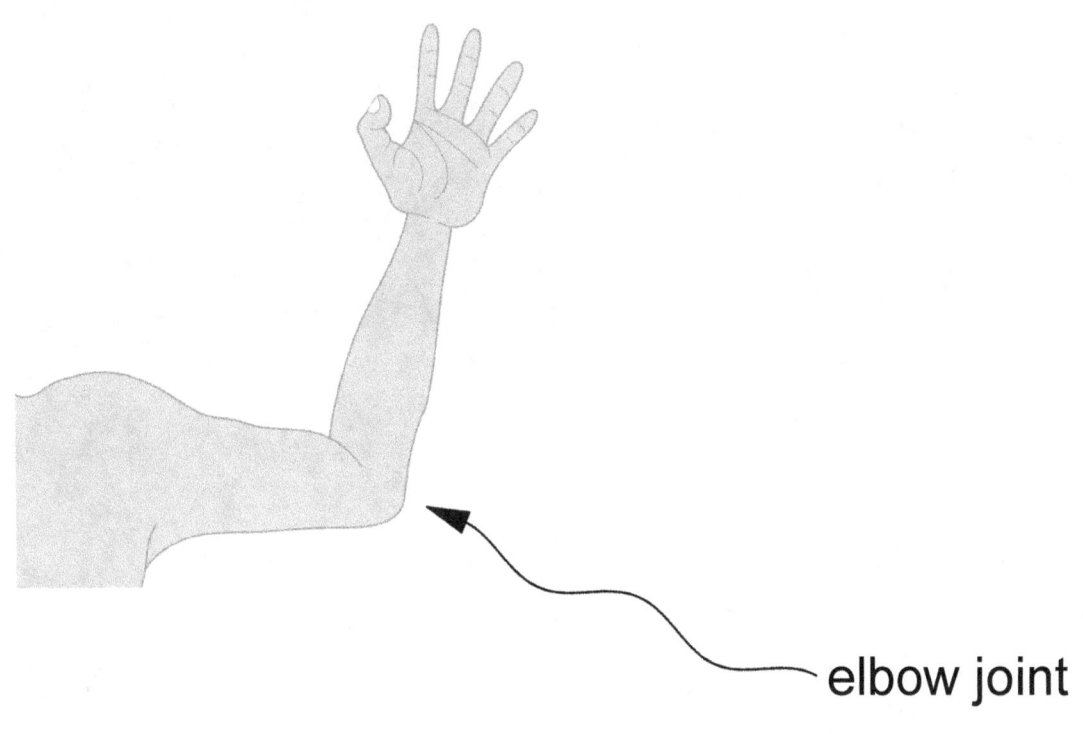

elbow joint

Cut out these pieces to form a body.

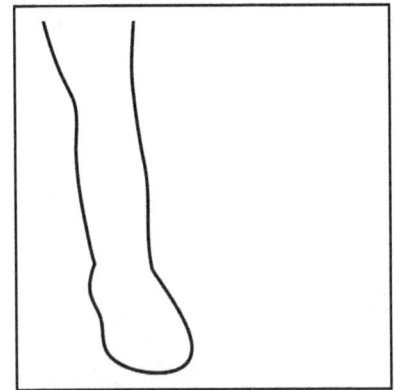
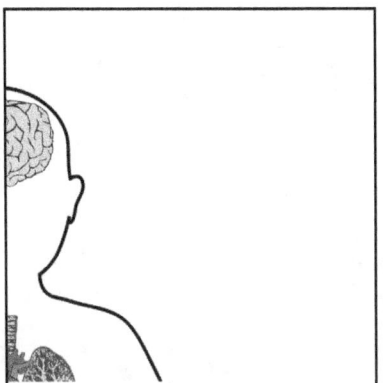
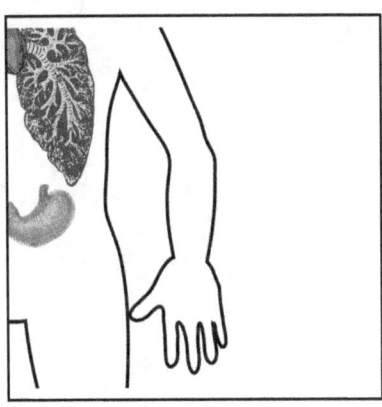
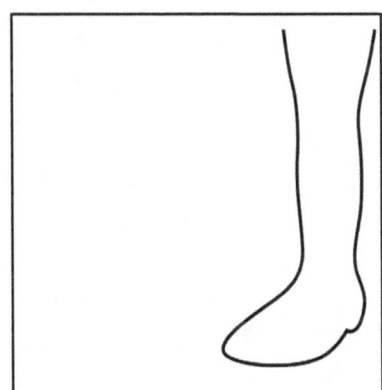
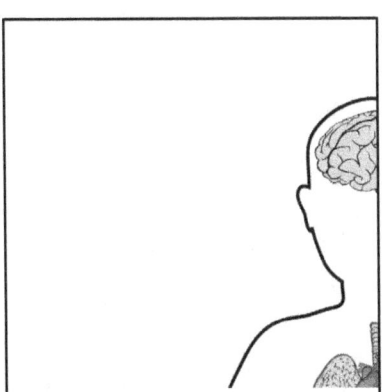
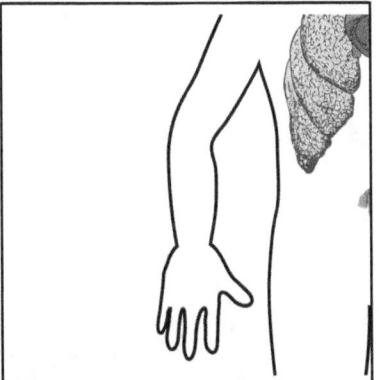

Can you spot the 6 differences between these two skeletons?

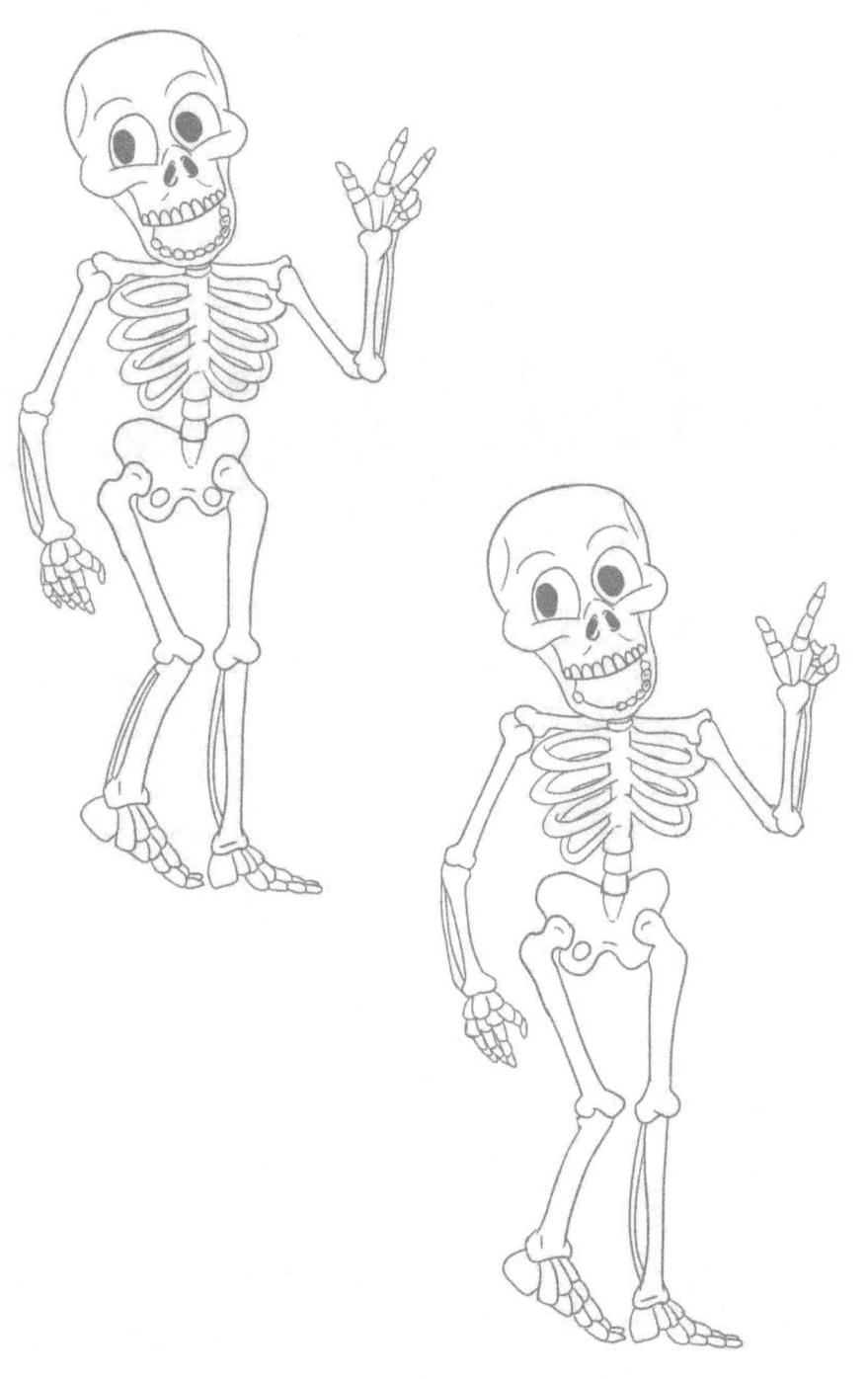

Put a cross if incorrect and put a check if correct.

- Bones help us stand upright

- There are 206 bones in our body

- Skeletons forms the bones in our body.

- Bones form the skeleton.

- The skeleton gives our body its shape.

- When bones meet it is called a point

- The place where 2 or more bones meet is called a joint.

Find the body parts hidden below:

M	N	S	E	Y	I	T	T	S	B	O	N	E	S
B	J	E	K	O	K	T	I	I	F	B	J	E	E
B	I	E	T	E	N	H	T	O	O	T	E	U	J
T	E	N	M	L	L	H	J	O	I	N	T	G	A
A	E	N	L	H	K	E	N	S	R	T	N	N	N
F	E	E	T	L	E	S	T	A	T	O	O	O	I
H	U	S	U	E	N	N	G	O	E	T	S	T	E
D	O	O	L	B	A	B	F	O	N	E	A	N	Y
M	O	U	T	H	I	N	G	I	O	N	I	H	E
I	T	E	B	E	L	H	E	B	N	A	L	N	S
N	I	B	S	T	S	S	A	O	R	G	E	J	L
N	T	B	S	G	N	U	L	B	E	S	E	I	I
E	S	E	H	E	A	R	T	T	N	T	L	R	A
M	S	S	E	O	R	R	H	C	A	M	O	T	S

blood	feet	lungs	skeleton
bones	fingers	mouth	stomach
brain	heart	nails	tongue
eyes	joint	nose	tooth

Our Body

THE HUMAN BODY

My Five Senses

Humans have five senses. Do you know what they are? Look at the pictures below and write the correct answers on the lines provided.

_____

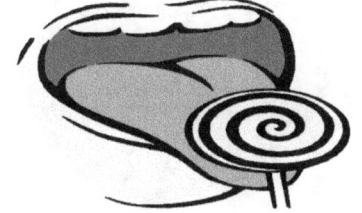

_____

_____

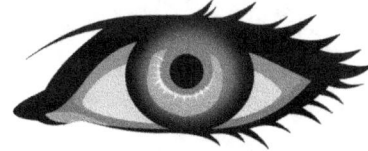

_____

_____

Match the body parts with the senses.

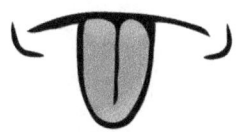   Sight

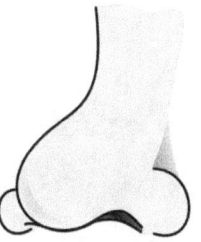   Hearing

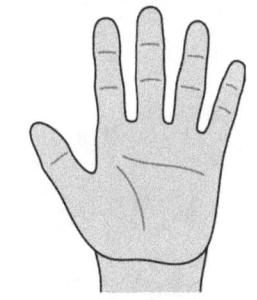   Taste

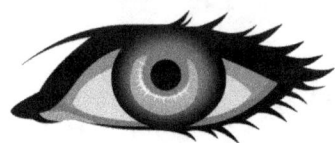   Touch

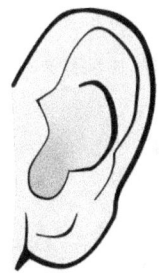   Smell

www.nolathenurse.com

Rewrite the sentences below:

1. see I my with eyes
   _____

2. colors see I different with eyes my
   _____

3. taste I food my tongue with
   _____

4. tongue my organ sense is a
   _____

5. tongue my me food helps taste my
   _____

6. smell I cannot nose my without
   _____

7. nose my helps smell things me
   _____

8. feel helps skin me my
   _____

Match the picture to its taste.

   Sweet

   Bitter

   Salty

   Sour

www.nolathenurse.com

Is this hot or cold? Write hot or cold below each picture.

Match the picture with the most suitable sense you would use.

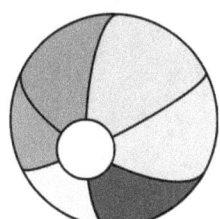

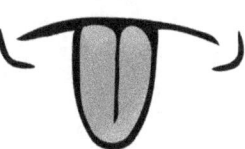

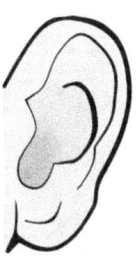

Fill in the blanks with the correct answer.

We can see things with our pair of _____.
We see objects of different colors, shapes and sizes.

Our _____ help us to read books.
We hear sounds with our pair of _____.
We hear loud and soft voices with our _____.
With our ears we _____ people laugh, talk and sing.
We smell with our _____.
We can _____ the flowers in our garden.
With our nose we can even _____ the garbage.
We can taste delicious food with our _____.
We can _____ hot or cold objects with our skin.
With our skin we can _____ rough and smooth objects.

        touch   noses   tongues   eyes
             ears   hear   smell

Fill in the crossword below:

Across:
2. I can ____ with my eyes
3. Your ____ can be used to listen to music.
4. This lime has a sour _____.
6. This is the largest sense organ.
7. Your ___ has taste buds on it to taste food.

Down:
1. Can you _____ the music playing?
3. We use these to see.
5. You use your nose to _____.
7. The sense that we use to tell is something is rough or smooth.
8. I can use my _____ to smell beautiful flowers.

www.nolathenurse.com

Our Body

THE HUMAN BODY

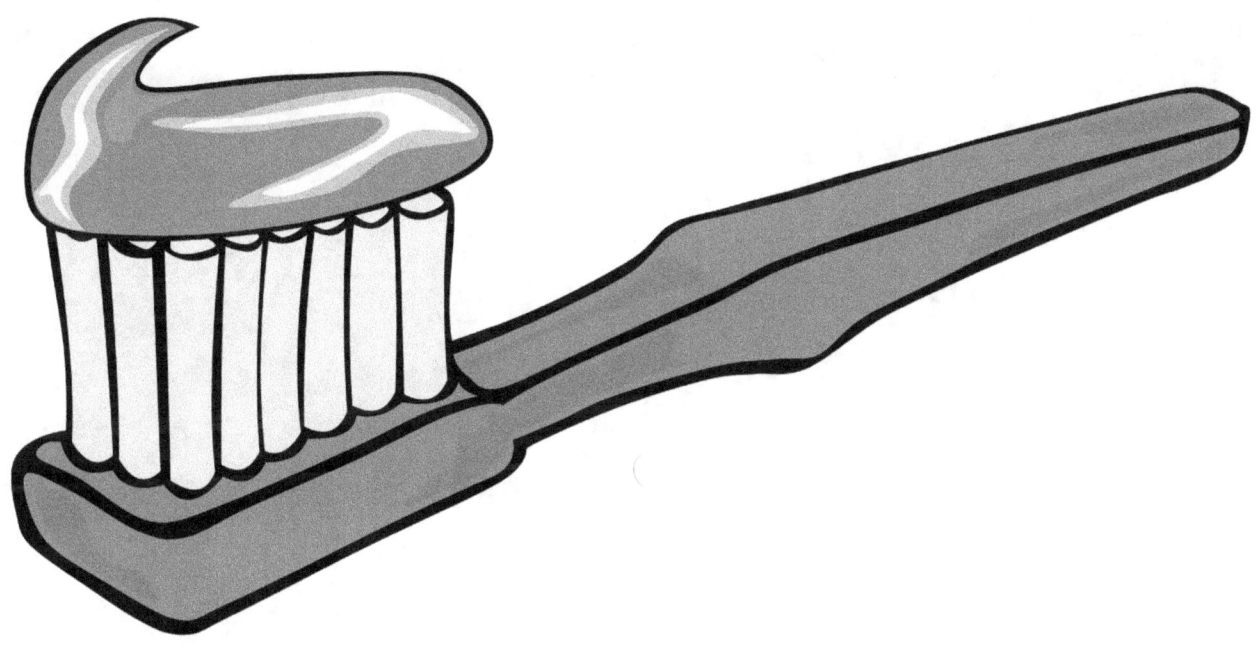

HOW TO TAKE CARE OF YOUR BODY

Assign the correct number to each picture.

1. Washing face
2. Bathing
3. Brushing teeth
4. Washing hands before and after a meal
5. Cleaning and cutting nails

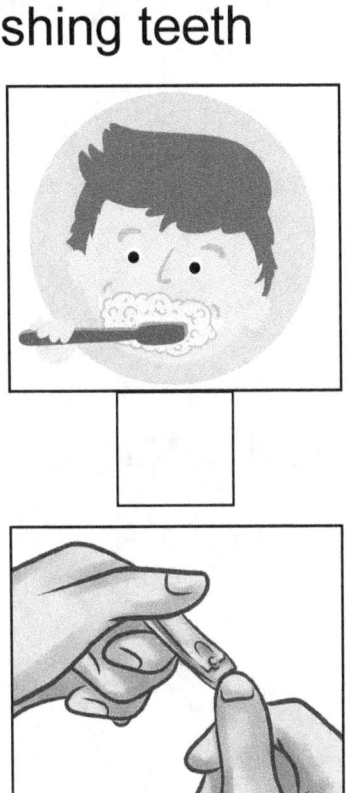

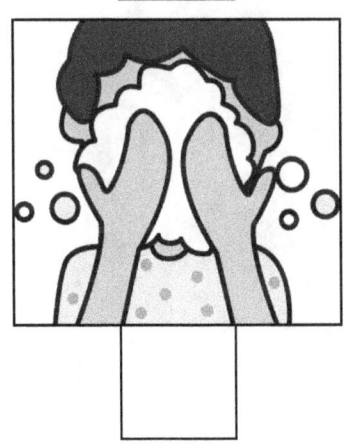

Shelly just woke up. Shelly has to wash her face and brush her teeth. Shelly has to go to the washroom. Can you help her get to the washroom?

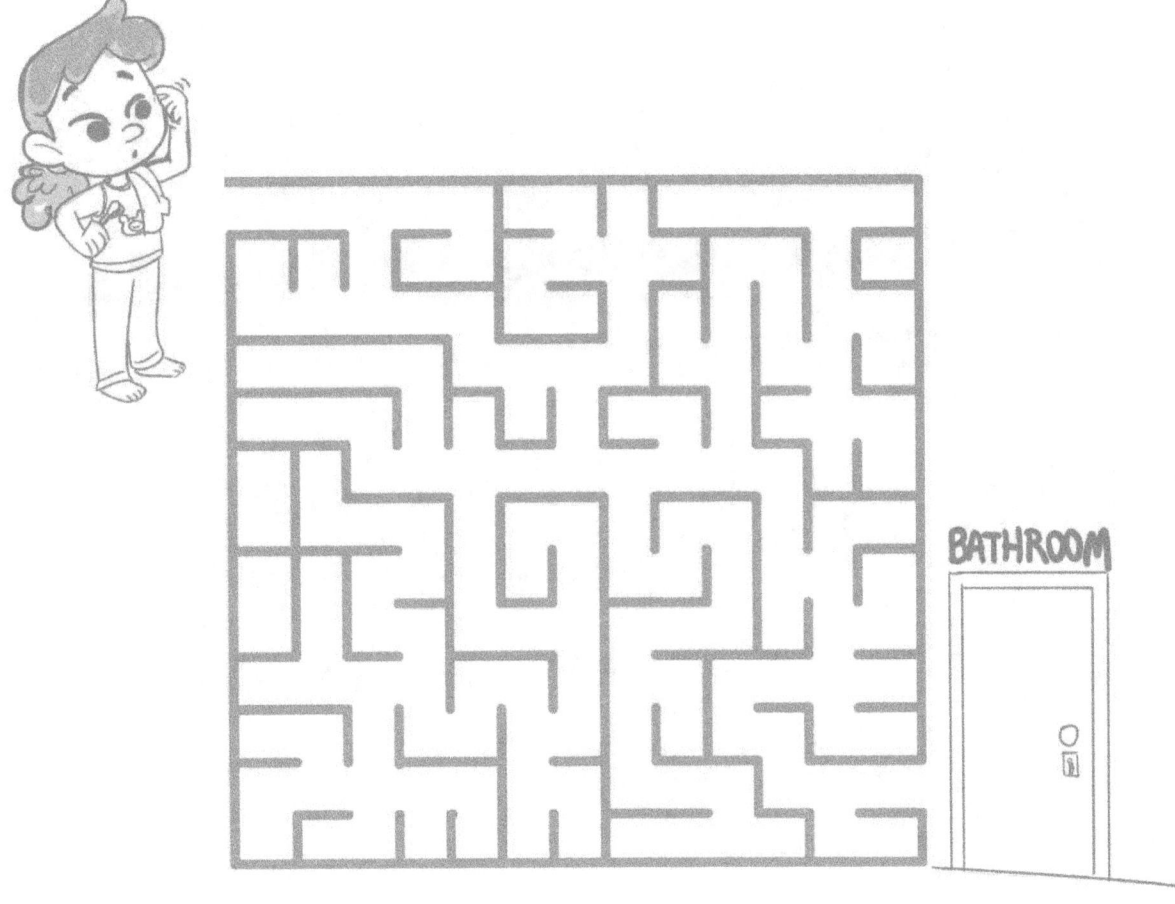

Do you take good care of your body? Write down 5 things you do to take care of your body.

1. _____

2. _____

3. _____

4. _____

5. _____

www.nolathenurse.com

Name the objects below: These objects help you keep your body clean.

 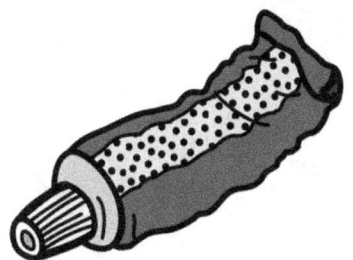 

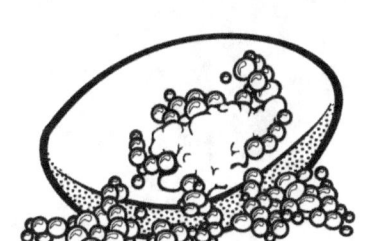  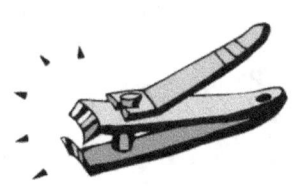

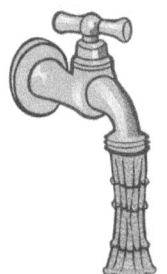

Circle the good habits in green.

Washing and scrubbing our body

Not combing your hair

Washing hands with soap and water

Wearing dirty clothes

Picking your nose

Cutting nails regularly

Biting nails

Eating with dirty hands

Not brushing your teeth

Having a bath

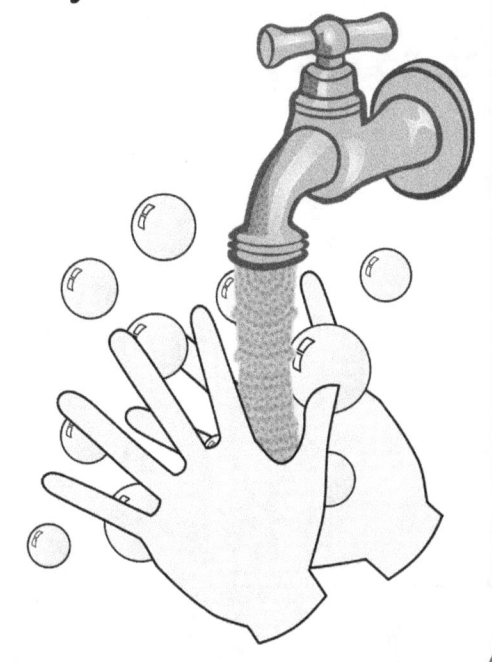

www.nolathenurse.com

Spot six (6) differences between the pictures below:

www.nolathenurse.com

Circle the bad habits you see in the picture below:

Which of these are Healthy Habits? Write 'HEALTHY' or 'UNHEALTHY' next to the habits listed below:

- Exercising regularly. _____

- Eating too much of candy. _____

- Eating fruits and vegetables. _____

- Drinking milk. _____

- Sleeping late. _____

- Sitting too close to the television. _____

- Having a good night sleep. _____

- Drinking plenty of water. _____

- Eating too much of ice-cream. _____

- Not having a bath regularly. _____

- Washing your hands before and after a meal. _____

Write the food items below in the correct column.

Broccoli Fries
Candy Chips
Chocolates Juice
Milk Fruits
Eggs Carrots
Fish

Healthy **Unhealthy**

_____ _____

_____ _____

_____ _____

_____ _____

_____ _____

These following free color sheets are placed here to help you get to know the characters from the Nola The Nurse® children's book series. Enjoy and pick up a copy of the hottest selling children's book in America that was recently featured on The Harry Show!

www.nolathenurse.com

Dr. Lawson Nurse Practitioner

Gumbo

Nola The Nurse®

Anita

Dr. Eden Nurse Practitioner

Answers

Page 2

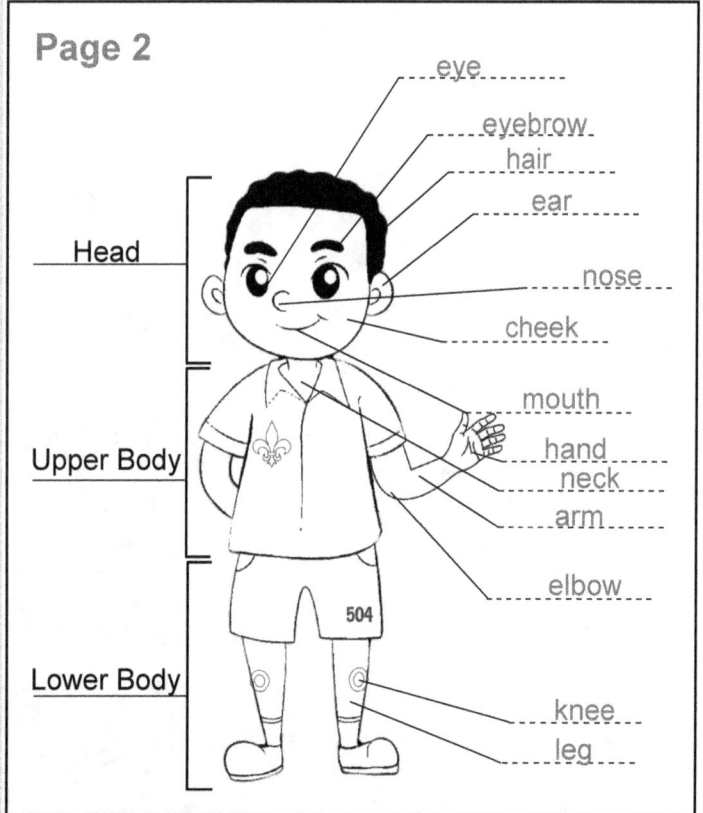

Head: eye, eyebrow, hair, ear, nose, cheek
Upper Body: mouth, hand, neck, arm, elbow
Lower Body: knee, leg

Page 3

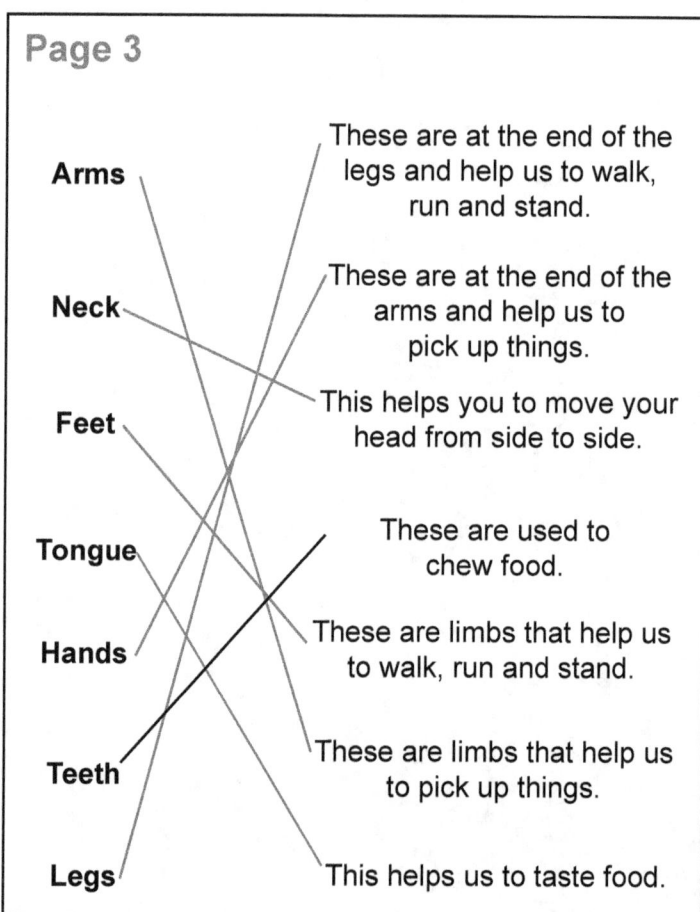

- Arms — These are limbs that help us to pick up things.
- Neck — This helps you to move your head from side to side.
- Feet — These are at the end of the legs and help us to walk, run and stand.
- Tongue — This helps us to taste food.
- Hands — These are at the end of the arms and help us to pick up things.
- Teeth — These are used to chew food.
- Legs — These are limbs that help us to walk, run and stand.

Page 6

Our body has three parts, the **Head**, **Upper Body**, and lower body.

The **Arm** has the **Hands** and fingers. The **Shoulders** connect the **Neck** with the upper body.

Page 8

- (Touch)
- (Write)
- Eat
- (Draw)
- Hear
- Kick

Page 9

- (Hop)
- (Walk)
- Eat
- Drink
- Talk
- See
- (Run)
- (Jump)

www.nolathenurse.com

Page 10

Nose

Hair

Tongue

Fingers

Foot

Eye

Neck

Mouth

Page 13

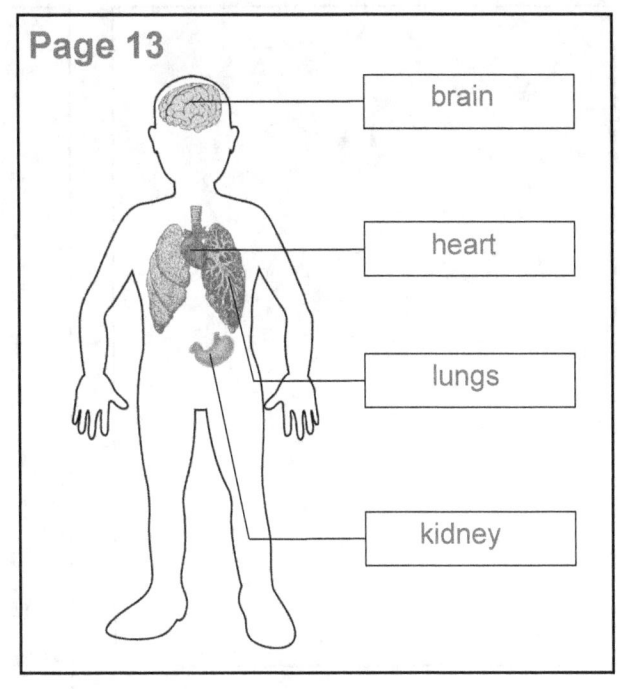

Page 14

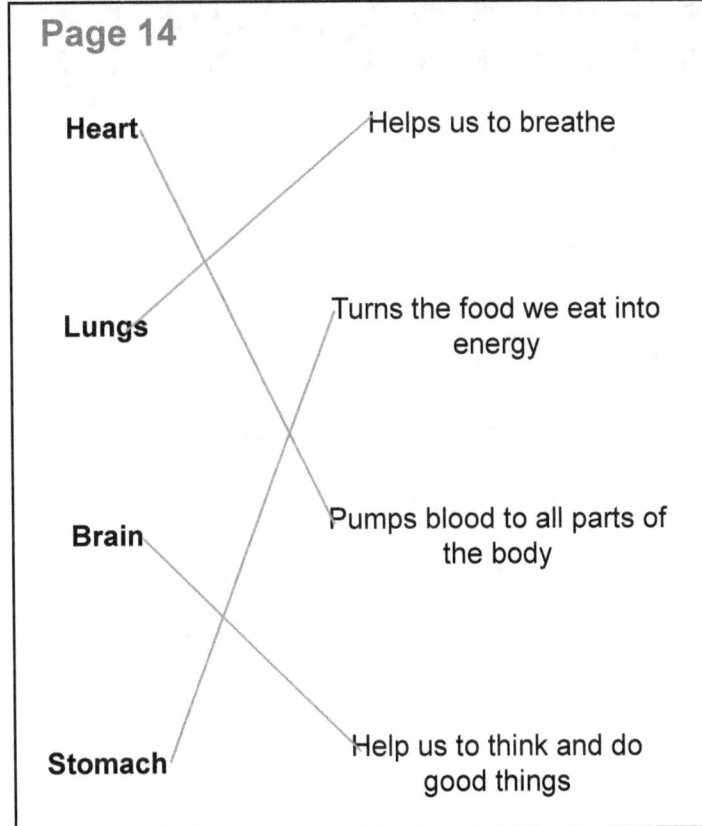

Heart — Helps us to breathe

Lungs — Turns the food we eat into energy

Brain — Pumps blood to all parts of the body

Stomach — Help us to think and do good things

Page 19

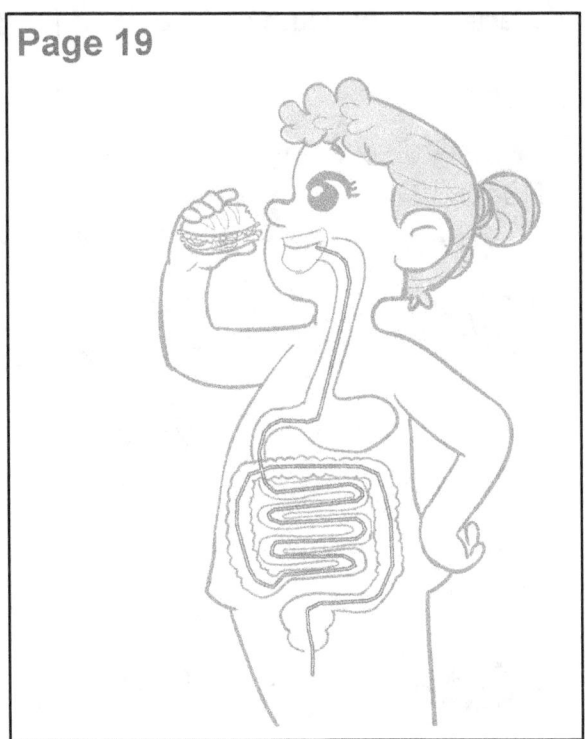

www.nolathenurse.com

Page 26

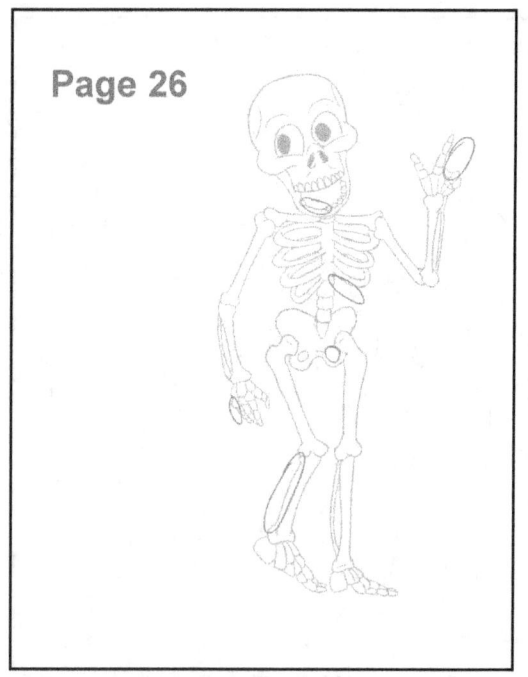

Page 29

hearing   sight

taste   touch

smell

Page 30

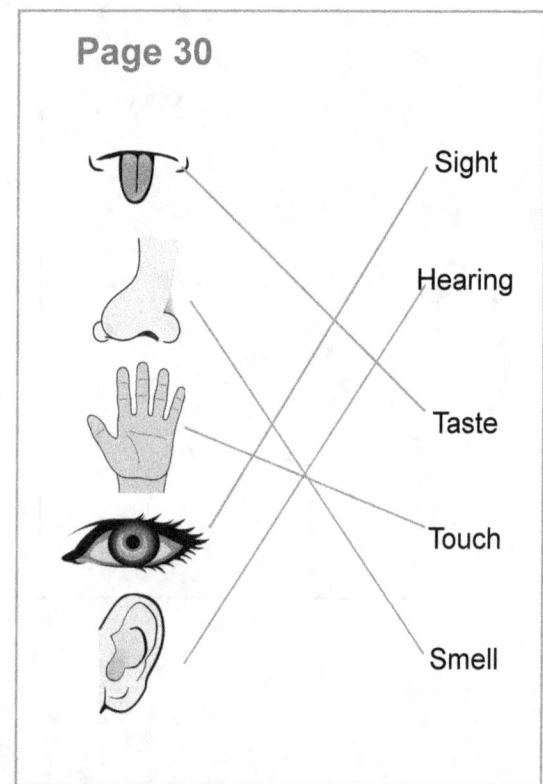

Page 28

Page 31

1. I see with my eyes.
2. I see different colors with my eyes.
3. I taste food with my tongue.
4. My tongue is a sense organ.
5. My tongue helps me taste my food.
6. I cannot smell without my nose.
7. My nose helps me smell things.
8. My skin helps me feel.

www.nolathenurse.com

Page 32

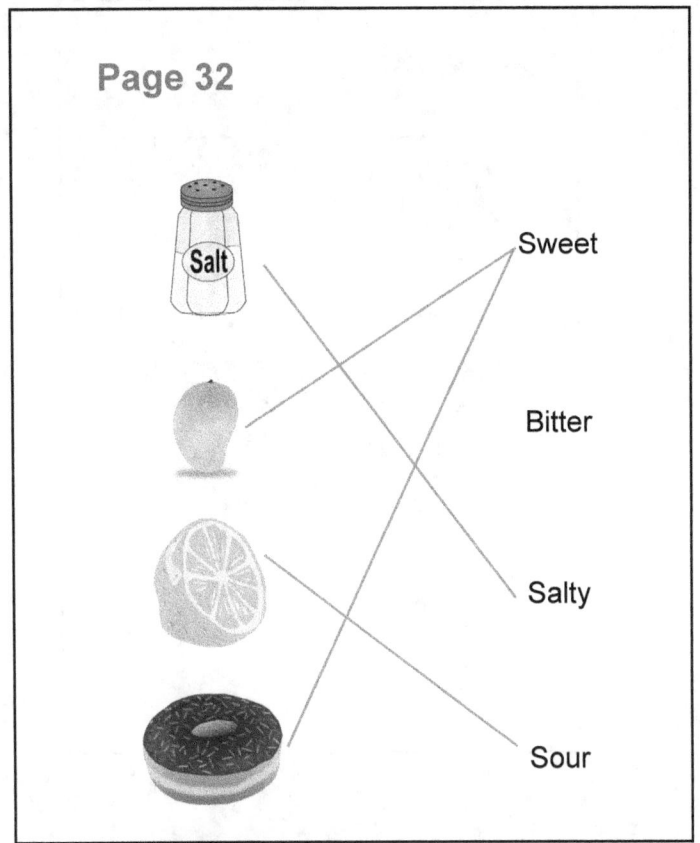

Page 33

Page 34

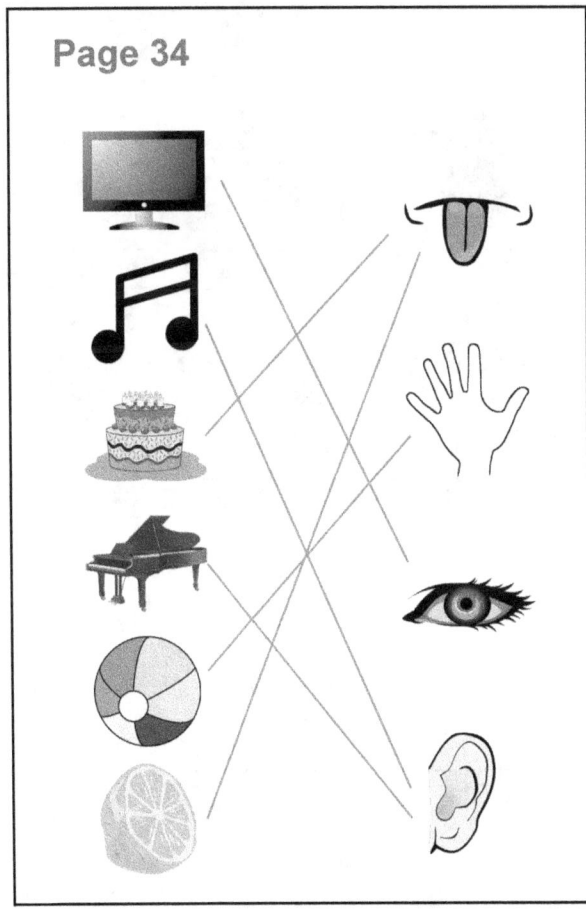

Page 35

We can see things with our pair of **eyes** .
We see objects of different colors, shapes and sizes.

Our **eyes** help us to read books.
We hear sounds with our pair of **ears** .
We hear loud and soft voices with our **ears** .
With our ears we **hear** people laugh, talk and sing.
We smell with our **noses**.
We can **smell** the flowers in our garden.
With our nose we can even **smell** the garbage.
We can taste delicious food with our **tongues**.
We can **touch** hot or cold objects with our skin.
With our skin we can **touch** rough and smooth objects.

www.nolathenurse.com

Page 36

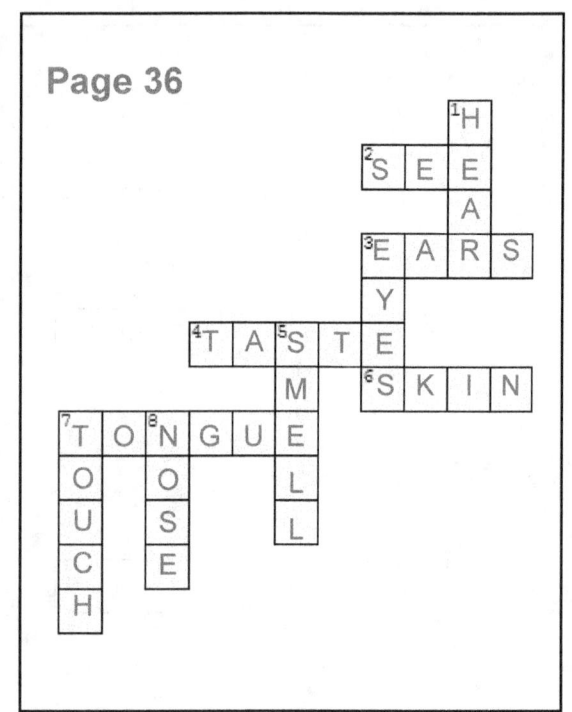

Page 37

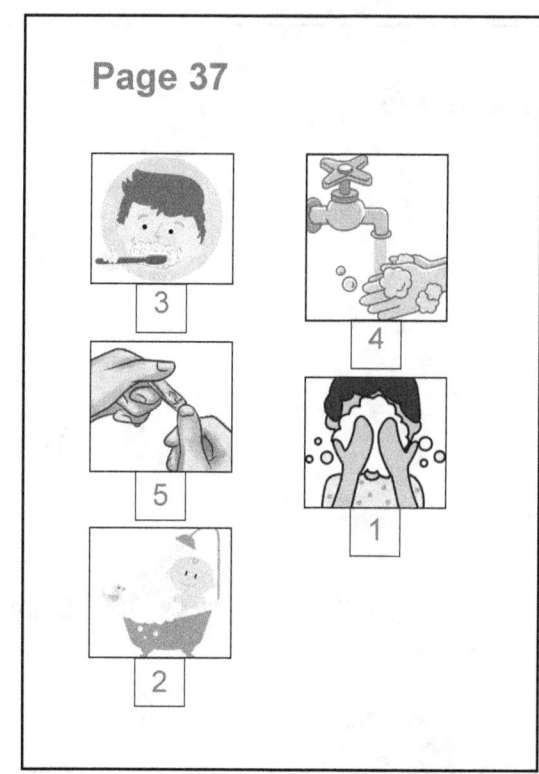

Page 38

Page 40

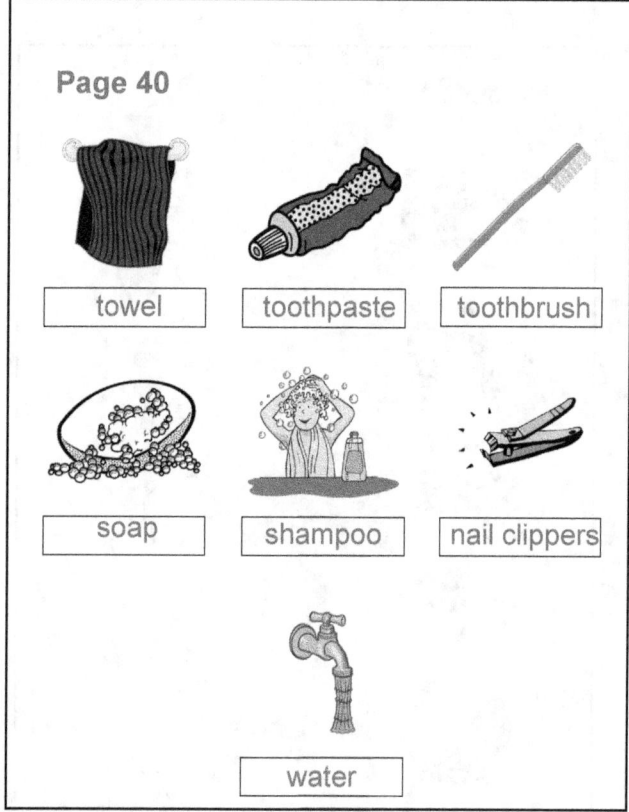

www.nolathenurse.com

Page 42

Page 44

Exercising regularly. _____HEALTHY_____

Eating too much of candy. _____UNHEALTHY_____

Eating fruits and vegetables. _____HEALTHY_____

Drinking milk. _____HEALTHY_____

Sleeping late. _____UNHEALTHY_____

Sitting too close to the television. _____UNHEALTHY_____

Having a good night sleep. _____HEALTHY_____

Drinking plenty of water. _____HEALTHY_____

Eating too much of ice-cream. _____UNHEALTHY_____

Not having a bath regularly. _____UNHEALTHY_____

Washing your hands before and after a meal. _____HEALTHY_____

Page 45

Healthy	Unhealthy
Broccoli	Candy
Milk	Chocolates
Eggs	Fries
Fish	Chips
Juice	
Fruits	
Carrots	

www.nolathenurse.com

Nola the Nurse

Maddi the Midwife

Bax the Nurse

Charo the CRNA

More books by Dr. Lawson

Nola The Nurse® She's On The Go Series Vol 1

Nola The Nurse® She's On The Go Series Vol 1 *Coloring Book*

Nola The Nurse® & Friends Explore The Holi Fest She's On The Go Series Vol 2

Nola The Nurse® & Friends Explore The Holi Fest She's On The Go Series Vol 2 *Coloring Book*

Nola The Nurse® Remembers Hurricane Katrina Special Edition

Nola The Nurse® Remembers Hurricane Katrina Special Edition *Coloring Book*

Nola The Nurse® Preschool Activity Book Vol 1

Nola The Nurse® Activity Book for Kindergarten Vol 2

Nola The Nurse® Math Worksheets for Kindergarten Vol 3

Nola The Nurse® English/Sight Word Workbook for Kindergarten Vol 4

Nola The Nurse® Math/English Worksheets for Preschoolers Vol 5

Nola The Nurse® Math Worksheets for First Graders Vol 6

Nola The Nurse® Explores STEM Activities Vol 7

Black Dot

www.NolaTheNurse.com
DrLawson@DrLawsonNP.com

About the Author

Dr. Scharmaine Lawson, NP is a nationally recognized and award-winning nurse practitioner in New Orleans, Louisiana. She has received numerous honors and awards for her contributions to healthcare in New Orleans since she became a family nurse practitioner in 2000, including the 2013 Healthcare Hero award (New Orleans City Business magazine) and 2008 Entrepreneur of the Year award (ADVANCE for Nurse Practitioner magazine). Dr. Lawson is a fellow in the American Association of Nurse Practitioners (FAANP) and a fellow in the American Academy of Nursing (FAAN).

After Hurricane Katrina, Dr. Lawson was instrumental in caring for the sick and disabled in New Orleans, where hospitals had closed and doctors had evacuated but never returned. Her patient load went from 100 to 500 in only three months. Thanks to her passion and unwavering dedication to caring for homebound patients in her home town, Dr. Lawson's story was featured on the CBS Evening News with Katie Couric.

Today, Dr. Lawson maintains a busy private practice in New Orleans by making house calls to the elderly and disabled who would otherwise not receive healthcare.

When this award-winning and nationally known nurse practitioner is not on the road delivering keynote speeches and attending various other media events, she loves reading to her children, Skylar Rose and Wyatt Shane.

www.DrLawsonNP.com
www.NolaTheNurse.com

www.ingramcontent.com/pod-product-compliance
Lightning Source LLC
Chambersburg PA
CBHW081724100526
44591CB00016B/2497